CW00401237

Smuggling Recipes

Carolyn Martin

Bossiney Books · Launceston

Author's acknowledgements

Thanks are due to the helpful staff at the Devon and Cornwall Record Offices, The Courtney Library at The Royal Institution of Cornwall and local libraries, who have given me direction and guidance, especially Mrs Christine North, the County Archivist at Cornwall Record Office.

The following titles from the Record Offices are some of the sources that I have used, although none of the recipes have been quoted in full: *Cornwall* – Tremayne of Heligan (TI363/1-20), Fortescue of Boconnoc (F(4)74 and 75), Howell of Ethy (HL(2)202), Rashleigh of Menabilly (R5682), Mary Dingle's Recipe Book (AM 1170), Antony House Records, Book I RBR and Part 1; *Devon* – Household and Hospitality recipes 1829-58 (74B/ME49-50), Recipe and cures book from Guppy of Sidbury 1820s-1840s (516M/F20), William Blake's recipe book 1783-85 (470/9).

I also consulted the Pendarves estate recipe book, signed by Ann Lanyon and Charity Hampton, and dated 1692 (the Royal Institution of Cornwall).

Finally, I must thank Ian, my husband, for his constructive criticism and for sampling the recipes with such enthusiasm.

Carolyn Martin
Carlidnack, Cornwall 1998

First published 1999 by Bossiney Books
Langore, Launceston, Cornwall PL15 8LD
Reprinted 2002

© 1999 Carolyn Martin

All rights reserved

ISBN 1-899383-12-3

Illustration acknowledgements

Cover photograph by Andrew Besley; artwork by Roger Fereday. The publishers are grateful to *different by design*, Truro, for allowing the use of their showroom

Printed in Great Britain by R. Booth (Troutbeck Press), Mabe, Cornwall

INTRODUCTION

Whilst chatting with a group of Cornish ladies recently, following a Christmas lunch in the village, I was surprised to hear that what they enjoyed most about the preparations for Christmas was not stuffing the turkey or icing the cake, but mixing up and sampling the brandy butter. It seems that the custom of lavishly sprinkling spirits into Christmas cooking lives on in the Westcountry.

This tradition dates back to the hey-day of smuggling, from about 1750-1850, when the recipe books of the time reflect the use and presumably abundance of best quality wine, rum and, above all, brandy. The recipes for stews use whole bottles of wine, not just a few spoonfuls, while cakes, puddings and desserts are enriched with cream, brandy and rum.

The way the spirit must have been poured into these dishes suggests that its presence could have been an embarrassment and it had to be consumed quickly, to avoid detection. What better way to hide the brandy than to cook with it and enliven the rather drab day-to-day diet of the time.

Living in the Westcountry in the eighteenth century was hard, with none of our modern comforts. London and the centre of government was remote, and taxes imposed to finance foreign wars were not popular. Smuggling was thought to be fair game, engaged in by rich and poor alike, with gains for all. The history and extent of smuggling have been well charted by many local historians, so the emphasis of this book is on recipes taken from the time when rum, brandy and wines were cheap, accessible and easily obtained in the cottage or manor house kitchen.

In short, this is an historical cookery book, with recipes that can be and, I hope, will be used today.

Smuggled ingredients

The quantity of brandy smuggled between 1750 and 1850 is almost unbelievable; in fact, the peninsula must have been awash with the spirit. It is said that in 1800 more brandy and rum were smuggled into the South West than was legally imported into the Port of London during the same year.

In 1770, 470,000 gallons of brandy are said to have been smuggled into Cornwall. Most of it came in the form of cognac from France and was brought in by small fishing boats, then hidden ashore in caves or other hiding places – private houses, churches (on weekdays only), inns or hotels. Sometimes it was even left out at sea, sunk along weighted lines to escape detection, to be collected later. There are many tales of hiding places and deceiving the Custom Men – of tubs of brandy being dug into the garden, hidden under false floorboards or even secreted under ladies' voluminous skirts.

Taxes on tea, salt, gin and rum led to similar undercover operations. Tea could be bought in Holland for seven pence a pound and sold in England for five to eight times as much. Gin also came in from the Low Countries and rum from the West Indies. Wine was smuggled when highly taxed, but when the tax was reduced in 1787, the smugglers switched to brandy. Better quality wines continued to be illegally imported after this date and much arrived via the frequent shipwrecks.

Surprisingly, sugar was regarded as a luxury or even as a medicine at this time. Queen Elizabeth I is said to have had black teeth caused by her taste for sweet things. Sugar was heavily taxed and, because of the price, the consumption of sugar or sugar candy was confined to the upper classes (honey was the usual sweetener for most people). Much of the imported cane sugar came from the West Indies and, although sugar beet was discovered as early as 1747, home-produced sugar beet was not manufactured economically until as late as 1919.

The main smuggled ingredients, then, were: brandy (cognac), geneva (gin), rum, red and white wines, port, sherry, whiskey (from Ireland rather than Scotland), tea, salt, coffee, cocoa and chocolate, and sugar.

Other ingredients

Eighteenth and nineteenth century Dorset, Devon and Cornwall saw an abundance of fresh fruit and vegetables, many varieties of meat and much fish. Coconuts and pineapples as well as other exotic fruits arrived unexpectedly in boats from the West and East Indies, either shipwrecked or trading from the ports and harbours. With the improved methods of land transport from the mid eighteenth century a much wider range of goods became available. However, some of the fruits and vegetables that we take for granted today were not available then. Tomatoes were just coming into general use at the end of the eighteenth century and bananas were not introduced into Britain until 1901, when the first shipload arrived in Bristol from Jamaica. Generally the rural population in the Westcountry would eat many locally produced vegetables (root and green), fruit (especially damsons and apples) and herbs. Salads on their own were not fashionable, but there was much pickling and preserving so that the produce could be enjoyed throughout the year.

Early cookery writers

Mrs Isabella Beeton with her *Book of Household Management* is probably the best known early cookery writer, but she was not the first and there were many before her, both male and female. One of the most useful of the earlier books, *The Art of Cookery made plain and easy*, published in London in 1747, was written by Hannah Glasse. She kept a shop in Covent Garden and worked as 'habit maker' to the Princess of Wales. Other writers include Elizabeth Raffald with *The Experienced English Housekeeper* (1769), John Farley, with *The London Art of Cookery* (1783),

Mistress Margaret (or Meg) Dods with her *Cook and Housewife's Manual* (1829), Eliza Acton with *Modern Cookery for Private Families* (1845) and Alexis Soyer with his *Modern Housewife* (1846).

These books bear little resemblance to our present day glossy, colourful cookery books; there were no indexes and many of the recipes had not been tried and tested, although Eliza Acton did make a point of saying that she had tried out all her recipes.

Often recipes were copied from earlier books without any acknowledgement. Although copies of cookery books would be kept only in the grander houses, many housewives had their own hand-written household books for recipes and remedies, either original or handed down from mother to daughter. Some of these have been placed at the County Record Offices.

Notes about ingredients and measurements

Most recipes in this book are for four people. Weights and measurements of ingredients have been adapted to modern imperial or metric standard. Use either imperial measurements or metric: don't mix them.

Spoon measurements:

1 tsp (teaspoon) = 5 ml   1 tbsp (tablespoon) = 15 ml.

For the sake of authenticity, butter is written into the recipes, although margarine could be used just as well. Unless stated otherwise, plain flour, rather than self-raising flour, has been used.

Generally dark rum gives a more robust flavour for cooking. White rum is a relative newcomer, because it was not marketed until 1862, but it can be used for lighter, sweet dishes. Best brandy or Cognac is ideal but other, cheaper brandies are equally acceptable, depending on the strength required and what you can afford. 40% proof brandy has been used in these recipes. Quantities can be varied, according to taste and occasion, provided the essence of the spirit is retained.

1824: Fowey Custom Men found brandy and wine aboard the *Union de Brest*. Later, when they searched the Mayor's home they discovered several more casks of brandy and wine, and the mayor himself was caught breaking up bottles of spirits, leaving the floor some three inches deep in alcohol.

SOUPS

Soups were the mainstay of cottage kitchen cooking, prepared over an open fire with fish, meat and vegetables in season. The recipe books of smuggling days, however, suggest more exotic and exacting preparations, enhanced with the last minute addition of wine, sherry or Madeira. Generally brandy and port are added to meat soups, wine to fish soups and cream to vegetable soups.

Crab soup, with dry sherry

Holiday makers coming to the Westcountry delight in sampling the local fresh crab sandwiches, soups and salads. Devon crabs are said to be particularly succulent and tasty.

Ingredients

8 oz (225 g) fresh, frozen or tinned crab meat
1 pint (575 ml) full cream milk
1 pint (575 ml) chicken or fish stock
2 oz (50 g) butter   2 oz (50 g) flour
1/4 tsp ground nutmeg   salt and pepper to taste
3 tbsp dry sherry   1/4 pint (150 ml) double cream
a few strands of saffron soaked overnight in hot water

Melt the butter in a large saucepan and add the flour, stirring before blending in the milk by degrees, followed by the stock. If necessary, whisk with a balloon whisk to remove any lumps. Add the spices and crab meat and bring to the boil. Simmer gently for about 15 minutes and, as a final touch, add the sherry and cream before serving.

Mock turtle soup

Towards the end of the eighteenth century, green turtles were shipped in from the West Indies, and turtle soup was produced at some of the grander dinner parties to impress wide-eyed guests. Not everyone could afford such luxuries, though, and mock turtle soup is an agreeable alternative, with the spices giving a hint of both the East and West Indies. Nutmeg especially was widely used in all spheres of cooking and became known as 'the English spice'. Mock turtle soup is traditionally served with forcemeat balls and decorated with orange and lemon slices.

Ingredients

2 pints (1.2 litres) meat stock
1 oz (25 g) medium oatmeal
1 stick of celery, 1 onion and 2 carrots
1 oz (25 g) long grain rice
1/2 tsp anchovy essence (optional)
1/2 tsp each pepper, mace, cinnamon, cloves, parsley and thyme
1/4 tsp cayenne pepper and 1 tsp salt
1 wine glass of sherry or Madeira (1/4 pint or 150 ml –
     Mrs Beeton suggests 1/4 bottle)
slices of orange and lemon for decoration

First of all prepare and chop the vegetables, then add to the stock with the herbs and spices. Sprinkle in the oatmeal, bring to the boil and simmer gently for about 1 1/2 hours. For the last 25 minutes of the cooking time, stir in the long grain rice and, when boiling, gently add the forcemeat balls (see page 15). Before serving, taste and if necessary add 1/2 tsp of anchovy essence. Finish with a large glass of sherry or Madeira.

Flat Poll soup (cream of cabbage soup)

Cabbage is one of the oldest vegetables and it is said that it was first cultivated in Dorset. Flat Poll is the name given to the dense white cabbage that used to be grown in such abundance in

Cornwall, although sadly smaller, more convenient varieties are now grown. It was mainly used as fodder for cattle, but many people in Cornwall still remember the delicious, sweet Flat Poll soup of their childhood. This recipe uses the dense Primo cabbage. It is a real cottage soup, which is greatly improved by the addition of brandy and cream, transforming a simple cabbage soup into haute cuisine.

Ingredients

1/4 hard, dense cabbage such as Primo, with the
    outer leaves removed
6 oz (175 g) cooked chicken or pork
2 slices of streaky bacon
2 pints (1.2 litres) chicken or ham stock
1 onion
salt and pepper
1 tsp sugar
1 sprig of rosemary, 2 bay leaves and 1 tsp dried mixed herbs
up to 1/4 pint (150 ml) or 1 glass of brandy or rum
1/4 pint (150 ml) single cream

Wash and prepare the vegetables, then slice the meat, cabbage and onion. Add to the stock with the herbs, sugar and seasonings, and simmer gently for about 1 1/2 hours until you have a warm, thick broth. When cooked check the seasoning, adding more salt if necessary, and finish with cream and a glass of best brandy or rum.

---

25 November 1720, *London Journal:* Unidentified wreck near Falmouth – 'a Dutch ship from Nantes run on shore near that port laden with brandy and saffron. She might have been got off but the country people coming so thick, they were obliged to leave her. But some of those plunderers having drank so much brandy and being so busy in the hold with a candle they set fire to the brandy by which means the ship and cargo were destroyed and two of the ruffians perished in the flames.'

FISH

As the Westcountry is surrounded by the sea, fish has always been the backbone of its cuisine. Local cookery books dating back to the seventeenth and eighteenth centuries have recipes for such fish as salmon, carp, sole, skate and sturgeon, together with many fish sauces. Cooked simply, nothing could be better.

Marinated herrings, pilchards or mackerel

It is generally thought that by salting and preserving pilchards when they were plentiful, fishermen's families in the past used to have a supply of fish to last through the winter. Unfortunately, the high price of salt (unless smuggled) made salting too expensive for most people and only small quantities of fish were salted down for winter use. Once the mainstay of the local fishing industry, pilchards (known locally as 'fair maids') are no longer caught in huge numbers.

Sousing or marinating herrings is another method of preserving fish and several smuggled ingredients could be used in a marinade: wine, tea, cochineal, spices and salt.

The following recipe is based on the ingredients suggested in a recipe book, dated 1692, from the Pendarves estate in Cornwall.

Ingredients

4 herrings
1 tsp salt, 1 tsp black pepper
1/4 tsp cochineal
1/2 tsp each of cloves and mace, 1 bay leaf for each fish
1/2 pint (275 ml) red wine (the original recipe suggests 4 pints!)
1/4 pint (150 ml) cold tea
1/4 pint (150 ml) vinegar

Begin by washing and cleaning the fish, cutting off the heads and tails and removing the main bones. There is no need to remove all the bones because these are softened with the long, slow cooking process. Next rub the salt, pepper, cochineal and other spices into the fish and place one bay leaf inside each herring. After that roll up into the usual roll-mop shape and place in an oven-proof casserole. Finally add the liquid, cover (traditionally with brown paper) and bake in a slow oven at 150°C/300°F/Gas 2 for 2¹/₂-3 hours. Leave until quite cold before removing the fish, now tinged slightly pink with the cochineal and red wine.

Sole bonne femme

French terms appear in cookery books from Medieval times onwards and 'bonne femme' is a dish cooked in a simple, peasant manner and generally served from the same casserole it was cooked in. In this recipe, local lemon sole is cooked with mushrooms and wine, although other white fish could be used with equal success.

Ingredients
1 lb (450 g) fresh lemon sole
1 oz (25 g) flour
1 large onion
6 oz (175g) mushrooms
¹/₂ pint (275 ml) fish stock
¹/₄ pint (150 ml)white wine
¹/₄ pint (150 ml) double cream
2 tbsp freshly chopped chives to finish

Prepare the fish by filleting and cutting into serving fillets, or ask the fishmonger to do this for you. Then place in a well buttered oven-proof dish and scatter with flour before adding the chopped onions and sliced mushrooms. Last of all pour in the stock and wine and bake in a moderate oven at 180°C/350°F/Gas 4 for 20 minutes. Before serving, add ¹/₄ pint (150 ml) double cream and scatter with freshly gathered, chopped parsley. Mashed potatoes and spinach make excellent accompaniments.

> 16 October 1774: unidentified wreck off the Isles of Scilly - her cargo of salt was seized by the Collector of Customs and placed in a warehouse. He had to call the military to assist in quelling the rioters and read the Riot Act.

Poached mackerel in a cheese and mustard sauce

Here a white béchamel sauce is flavoured with cheese, mustard and brandy. Most recipes for mackerel suggest grilling the fish, but poaching in a court bouillon or flavoured stock is just as good.

Ingredients
4 mackerel, trimmed and filleted

For the court bouillon
1 carrot, 1 onion and 1 stick of celery
bay leaf, few parsley stalks and 12 pepper corns
5 fl oz (150 ml) wine vinegar
1 pint (575 ml) water

For the béchamel sauce
1 pint (575 ml) milk
2 oz (50 g) butter
2 oz (50 g) flour
2 cloves, salt and pepper
1 scant tbsp freshly made English mustard
4 oz (110 g) Cheddar cheese (grated)
1 fl oz (25 ml) brandy or rum

Prepare the court bouillon, adding the peeled and chopped vegetables to a pan of water. Bring to the boil and simmer for 15 minutes. Then leave to cool before straining and pouring over the prepared mackerel, in a wide and shallow pan. Next, simmer the mackerel very gently for about 15 minutes. Alternatively, the fish can be baked in a moderate oven for a similar length of time. Remove from the court bouillon before serving.

Whilst the fish is cooking make the béchamel sauce: melt the butter in a small pan, then add all the flour, followed by the milk in stages. Remember to stir to prevent lumps forming, whisking if necessary, and bring to the boil. Continue cooking gently for about 15 minutes, again stirring frequently. Last of all add the grated cheese and freshly made English mustard and the brandy or rum.

The mackerel can be placed on individual plates or on one large serving dish, pouring the béchamel sauce over each fish and scattering with chopped parsley or fennel to decorate.

Buttered crab

A traditional recipe for one of the best loved of all Westcountry shellfish.

Ingredients
4 oz (110 g) white crabmeat (fresh, frozen or tinned)
2 anchovy fillets
1/4 pint (150 ml) dry white wine
3 tbsp fresh white breadcrumbs
1/4 tsp nutmeg, salt and pepper to taste
3 oz (75 g) butter
2 slices of hot buttered toast and chopped chives to garnish

Chop and pound the anchovies and add to the wine with the breadcrumbs and spices. Select a suitable pan for the ingredients, then bring to the boil and simmer for about 5 minutes. Meanwhile mix the crab with the butter and add to the hot wine mixture. Cook together for a further 5 minutes. Serve immediately on hot buttered toast, garnishing with freshly chopped chives.

> 1783: A Polperro-based ship was detained off Lundy by *HMS Beaver* and was caught smuggling: 119 bags containing 6,632 lb tea, 242 casks with 2,224 gallons of brandy, and 90 casks with 834 gallons of gin.

MEAT

In the past fresh meat was readily available for those who could afford it, from venison, pheasant, chicken, turkey, mutton and lamb, beef, ham and pork to the humble rabbit. Most meats improve when marinated in rum or brandy or casseroled in wine – this must have been especially true in the eighteenth and early nineteenth century when spirits were so cheap and plentiful.

Westcountry roast goose

The traditional Christmas goose is coming back into fashion, with roast turkey seeming almost everyday fare. Goose has never been out of favour in Tavistock, Devon, where the annual Goosey Fair is celebrated on the second Wednesday in October. There is a goose market where geese are sold, and roast goose dinners and sandwiches are served in the town throughout the day.

Traditional accompaniments for goose are as for duck, with sage and onion stuffing, apple sauce, potatoes and green peas. An original suggestion from the Westcountry is to serve roast goose with glazed turnips, cooked in butter and brown sugar.

Ingredients

10 lb (4.5 kg) goose
1 pint (575 ml) dry cider
2 fl oz (50 ml) dark rum
salt and pepper

There are many modern methods of preparing goose. I usually pierce the skin and pour boiling water over the bird, then allow it to dry before roasting. This ensures a crisp finish.

Much fat is collected during the roasting process and so there is no need to add extra fat, although in the Westcountry fashion 1 pint (575 ml) of cider can be added to the roasting tin and the goose basted with the liquid from time to time. Salt and pepper should be rubbed over the body before filling with the chosen stuffing and roasting at 220°C/425°F/Gas 7 for 30 minutes. Then the oven should be reduced to 180°C/350°F/Gas 4 for about 2½ hours. The remaining cider can be poured over the bird towards the end of the roasting time, to crisp the skin.

Mrs Beeton's recipe for gravy to accompany roast goose is made from 1 tsp dry mustard, a 'saltspoonful' of salt, a few grains of cayenne pepper and a glass of port wine, which should be added to the stock with the fat removed.

A 'smuggled' stuffing can be made by soaking 4 sliced eating apples in ¼ pint (150 ml) rum overnight. The next morning add: 4 oz (110g) fresh breadcrumbs, 1 chopped onion, several sage leaves, ½ tsp mace and the sliced goose liver. Stir until the stuffing is well blended and use to stuff into the cavity of the goose, or cook separately.

As a final flourish, one book of old Cornish recipes suggests that you should pour a ladleful of rum over the bird and set it alight as you bring it to the table.

Forcemeat balls

Ingredients
4 oz (110 g) breadcrumbs
1 oz (25 g) chopped suet
1 tbsp freshly chopped parsley
1 tsp mixed dried herbs
¼ tsp grated nutmeg
1 beaten egg, for mixing
grated rind from one lemon
salt and pepper to taste
1 tbsp brandy

Begin by mixing the dry ingredients and then add enough egg and brandy to bind the mixture together. Finally, form into about 12 balls and poach in, for example, mock turtle soup (see page 8) for 25 minutes.

Dorset jugged steak

Like jugged hare, the steak is cooked in a covered casserole. Here the red wine and beetroot add especial richness. There are many recipes for beef stews in the local archives, one of which suggests cooking the beef with a pint of port. To be fair, port was the cheapest foreign wine, with only a nominal duty to be paid and so was not worth smuggling.

Ingredients
2 lb (900 g) shin of beef
1 oz (25 g) flour
1 oz (25 g) beef dripping or cooking oil
1/2 pint (275 ml) red wine and 3/4 pint (425 ml) beef stock
1 onion and 4 oz (110 g) cooked beetroot
1 tsp dried mixed herbs, 3 cloves and salt and pepper

Discard any unwanted fat from the beef and cut into cubes. Melt the dripping in a heavy-based casserole, and fry the beef quickly in the fat. Reduce the heat and sauté the onion until lightly browned. Stir in the flour and gradually add the beef stock, then the red wine, herbs and spices.

Bring to the boil and transfer to an ovenproof casserole and cook in a slow oven at 150°C/300°F/Gas 2 for 1 1/2 to 2 hours, adding the cooked beetroot after the first hour. More liquid may have to be added during the cooking time. Dorset jugged steak is usually served with potatoes and carrots.

> 1750 Robert Heath, an officer on St Mary's, Isles of Scilly wrote:
> 'Commanders and Passengers of Ships from the West Indies, or other foreign parts, putting in, never fail of shewing their Liberality, and of leaving some of their commodities and Riches behind them.
> By this means the Islanders are supplied with a Stock of Rum, Brandy, Wine and other foreign Liquors, some for consumption upon the Island, and some (by leave of the Custom House) for consumption elsewhere.'

Fricassée of chicken, with dates and gooseberries

Eighteenth-century recipes use many French terms; a 'fricassée' is a white stew cooked in wine and stock, then thickened with egg yolks and cream just before serving. The addition of gooseberries, raisins and dates is unusual, but this particular medley of ingredients appears in a seventeenth-century recipe book from the Pendarves estate in Cornwall.

Ingredients

6 chicken joints
1 pint (575 ml) chicken stock
1 oz (25 g) butter
1 oz (25 g) flour
1/2 pint (275 ml) dry white wine
2 medium onions sliced
1 bouquet garni
1/2 tsp nutmeg, pepper and salt
1 tsp sugar
handful of gooseberries
6 dates, stoned
4 oz (110 g) raisins

To finish

2 egg yolks
1/4 pint (150 ml) single cream

Brown the chicken and onions in the melted butter, then stir in the flour and add the stock and wine, together with the seasonings, gooseberries, dates and raisins. Bring to the boil and cook gently for about an hour.

Before serving, skim off any unwanted fat, blend the cream with the egg yolks and mix with a little of the warm stock before adding to the chicken. The dates and raisins give a dark splash of colour to the chicken.

Serve with a surround of saffron rice and peas.

Rabbit with prunes

A real country dish, tasting almost like chicken. Nowadays, prepared and jointed rabbits are sold at most large supermarkets.

Ingredients
1 rabbit, about 2¹/2 lb (1.1 kg) in weight, ready prepared and
    cut into serving joints
1 tsp mixed herbs
¹/2 pint (225 ml) red wine
4 oz (110 g) bacon
2 tbsp olive oil
2 tbsp flour
3 onions
1 bay leaf
1 tsp French mustard
2 tbsp dark rum
8 oz (225 g) pitted (stoned) prunes, soaked
    in ¹/2 pint (250 ml) red wine

Marinate the rabbit in the herbs and red wine in the refrigerator for 24 hours. Fry the chopped bacon lightly in a heavy based saucepan. Drain and dry the rabbit pieces, dipping them into the seasoned flour before frying with the bacon. Remove both the bacon and the rabbit, add the onions and fry lightly.

Return the rabbit and bacon to the pan with the onions and add the remaining ingredients, including the marinade, the prunes and wine. Bring to the boil and simmer gently for about 2 hours or until the rabbit is tender. Season to taste and stir in the rum just before serving, allowing the liquid to warm through. Creamy mashed potatoes and a green vegetable go nicely with this dish.

Pork with brandy, apples and cream

If the following anecdote from *The Dorset County Chronicle* has any truth, this recipe must come from Dorset: 'There is a story told in Portland regarding the expression still used "stick to the pork Archie", which came about as a result of this wreck [in 1868 the ship *Bank* was wrecked off Portland Bill]. As the *Bank* started to break up, barrels of pickled pork (amongst other items) commenced floating clear. Samuel Archie, a local inhabitant, plunged into the sea after them, whilst his wife Molly kept shouting at him from the cliff, "Stick to the pork Archie, never mind anything else, stick to the pork." '

Ingredients

1 lb (450 g) pork fillet	1 tsp crushed rosemary
salt and pepper	lemon juice
2 oz (50 g) butter	2 eating apples
1/4 pint (150 ml) double cream	2 tbsp brandy or whiskey

Trim the pork, removing any surplus fat, and cut into about twenty even-sized serving pieces. Then sprinkle with the salt, pepper, chopped rosemary and lemon juice. Leave to marinate for at least half an hour.

Heat the butter in a frying pan and add the pork, frying for a few minutes until well browned – about 4 minutes on each side. Reduce the heat, add the cored and cubed apples, cover with a lid and cook the pork for a further 5 minutes on each side. In another small pan, warm the brandy, set it alight (taking care with the flames) and pour over the pork.

Finally add the cream and let it simmer for a few minutes. Serve the pork topped with the apples and surround with the sauce.

Accompany with mashed potatoes and any green vegetable.

1764, *Exeter Flying Post*: Great quantities of foreign teas, brandy and other manufactures are daily imported into this kingdom from Scilly, where boats generally intercept all ships passing by there in their course up both Channels, under pretence of furnishing them with greens, poultry etc.

VEGETABLES AND STUFFING

During the Georgian period (1714-1837) a wide variety of vegetables were eaten. Colour and presentation were important and spinach, tansy and beetroot in particular were valued for their strong colours and flavours. Potatoes, greens and other root vegetables were often the staple diet of the less well off, whereas the aristocracy could afford to buy unusual and exotic varieties of vegetables raised by the estate gardeners, under glass out of season. Cucumbers were a case in question and whole cucumbers were often served stewed or stuffed with fried onions, or oven-baked with spices and red wine.

Pickled cucumbers

There is a detailed recipe for pickled cucumbers in the hand-written recipe book dated 1785 belonging to William Blake from South Devon. Salt and spices were taxed at that time, so they could have come from a smuggled source.

Ingredients
3 cucumbers, sliced – spiky, ridged cucumbers are best
4 onions, peeled and chopped
4 level tbsp coarse salt

Wash the cucumbers, cut into slices and into half again if too large. Peel and chop the onions. Sprinkle the cucumbers and onions with the salt and leave to stand in a bowl overnight. This removes any excess water which might dilute the vinegar. The next morning drain and wash to remove the salt, then dry well. Pack into jars and cover with cold spiced vinegar.

Spiced vinegar
2 pints (1.2 litres) malt vinegar
1 onion
1 tsp salt
1 oz (25 g) mixed pickling spices

Tie the spices into a piece or bag of muslin and boil the vinegar in a covered pan with the salt and onion for 5 minutes. Leave until cold before removing the spices and onion, then pour over the cucumber.

Note To avoid boiling the vinegar and spices, ready-prepared pickling vinegar can be bought. If a very mild pickle is preferred, omit the overnight salting process.

Glazed parsnips

A seventeenth-century country house recipe for parsnips suggests boiling the parsnips in the usual way, then coating with a glaze made from:

1¹/2 oz (40 g) melted butter
1 tsp honey
2 tbsp orange and the same of lemon juice
¹/4 tsp each of ground cinnamon and nutmeg
salt and pepper to taste
1 tbsp sherry or Madeira
1 tbsp chopped coriander

Warm the ingredients together and pour over the cooked parsnips. Scatter with 1 tbsp of fresh chopped coriander to serve.

---

4 January 1817: The Brig *Resolution* homeward bound for London, with a cargo of wines and oranges from Oporto, was driven on to the beach at Porthleven.
The tinners and fishermen, together with most of the population from Porthleven to Prussia Cove, raided the cargo and within an hour there was a regular riot.
The troops arrived, but they could not stop the looting.
Many died of alcoholic posioning or drowned.
It is said the wine found its way into the cellars of the local gentry and births and marriages were toasted in 'Old Resolution' for many years.

1701, *Dorset Magazine:* Wreck of the *Katherine*, Isle of Portland – 'some of the country people did not only imbezle and carry away the chesnutts, but beat and abuse the officers in the execution of their dutyes.'

Chestnut and brandy stuffing

This is a recipe adapted from a book of old Cornish recipes. Traditionally chestnut stuffing was used for fish, especially mackerel, but it also goes well with the Christmas turkey.

Ingredients
8 oz (225 g) cooked chestnuts (boiled and peeled)
2 oz (50 g) fresh breadcrumbs
1 oz (25 g) melted butter
2 tbsp clotted cream
2 tbsp brandy
1 tsp lemon juice
1/4 tsp nutmeg

Ready-prepared chestnut purée can be substituted for the fresh chestnuts, but the results are usually inferior.

First, melt the butter in the small pan, add the mashed chestnuts and other ingredients. Then cook in a moderate oven for 15-20 minutes at 180°C/350°F/Gas 4.

Spinach with raisins and almonds

In the past, almonds were more widely used than they are today in both savoury and sweet dishes. Imported from southern Europe, they were expensive luxury items and the poor could only afford them for celebration meals such as at Christmas or Easter time; during Lent, when meat was forbidden, almonds provided a useful source of protein. They could be ground, for use in puddings and butters, eaten whole after a meal or, as here, lightly cooked with spinach and rum-soaked raisins.

Ingredients
1¹/₂ lb (675 g) fresh spinach
1 oz (25 g) butter
1 clove of garlic, crushed
1 onion, chopped finely
¹/₂ oz (15 g) flaked almonds
2 oz (50 g) raisins, 2 fl oz (50 ml) rum
salt and pepper

Soak the raisins overnight in the rum, or for at least 2 hours. Cook the spinach in a little water until tender (about 15 minutes), then drain well. Melt the butter in another saucepan and fry the garlic and onion lightly. Add the spinach, almonds and raisins with any remaining rum and cook gently for 10 minutes. Adjust the seasoning to taste, and serve.

PUDDINGS

When I was looking through the hand-written recipe books in the local archives, I came across an endless number of recipes for creams and custards, puddings and pies.

Some suggest rose or orange flower water as a flavouring. Others specify rum or brandy, as with the next recipe for almond cream, where the somewhat bland taste of ground almonds is enhanced by the sharper brandy.

Today almonds are generally associated with Christmas, but they used to feature far more widely in the recipe books of the Great Houses: 'marchpane' was the name for the elaborately decorated marzipan centre-piece at Elizabethan banquets. Sometimes highly expensive gold leaf was used in the decoration.

> In 1800 the naval cutter *Dover* seized the *Endeavour* of Bideford off Brandy Cove, Ilfracombe, with her cargo of 1,076 gallons of brandy, 500 of gin and 225 of rum.

Almond cream

A typical recipe, taken from a number of Westcountry sources.

Ingredients

1 pint (575 ml) single cream	4 eggs
1/4 tsp nutmeg	1 blade of mace
1 tbsp rose water	3 tbsp brandy
grated rind from 1/2 lemon	4 oz (110 g) sugar
4 oz (110 g) ground almonds	

cinnamon and spoonfuls of raspberry purée for decoration

Mix together the beaten eggs, cream, sugar, almonds and flavourings in a double boiler (or in a large oven-proof jug or basin in a pan of boiling water).

Leave the mixture to thicken and cook whilst you are getting on with something else in the kitchen. Just remember to whisk and stir now and again. Then add 1 tbsp of rose water and 3 tbsp of brandy before pouring into dainty glass dishes. Allow to cool before serving and decorate with a sprinkling of cinnamon and swirls of raspberry purée.

Saffron syllabub

In Elizabethan times, syllabub was a drink of fresh foaming milk (often straight from the cow) flavoured with wine.

Later brandy, sherry and sugar were added to the cream and by the eighteenth century the syllabub had developed into a more substantial syllabub trifle – a layer of fruit and sponge, covered with syllabub. Sometimes it was flavoured with cochineal or saffron, which is now said to be the most expensive spice in the world. What could be more appropriate for the Westcountry than a recipe with saffron, cream, smuggled French wine and 'Cousin Jack', the local name for cognac?

Today, quick and simple to prepare, syllabub remains a popular sweet and, as it improves with standing, it can be made well in advance, adding a final flourish to a party.

Ingredients
6 tbsp sweet white wine
1 lemon, 2 tbsp brandy
few strands of saffron
3 oz (75 g) caster sugar
10 fl oz (275 ml) double cream
macaroons or ratafias to accompany

Grate the lemon and squeeze out the juice. Add the wine, brandy and saffron, and leave to stand for several hours or overnight. Strain the liquid into another bowl and stir in the sugar, then the cream. Whisk the mixture until it forms soft peaks and spoon into small pretty glass bowls, with a plate of macaroons or ratafias alongside.

Devonshire junket

The earliest recipe for a junket dates from 1653 but, with the production of commercial rennet in bottled form in the 1870s, it became a popular Victorian nursery sweet. The secret with junkets is to add the rennet to the milk at the right temperature, not too hot or too cold.

Ingredients
1 pint (575 ml) fresh milk
1 tbsp sugar
2 tbsp brandy
3 tsp rennet (vegetarian rennet is available if preferred)
5 fl oz (150 ml) clotted cream
nutmeg or cinnamon to flavour and decorate

Place the sugar and brandy in a cool serving bowl. Warm the milk to blood heat (37^0C or 98.4^0F), then add to the other ingredients in the bowl. Stir in the rennet (too much rennet will give a salty taste) and leave to set in a cool place – not in the refrigerator. Spoon clotted cream over the surface to serve. Decorate and flavour with either nutmeg or cinnamon.

White-pot or saffron bread and butter pudding

Although bread and butter pudding (originally known as white-pot) has appeared in recipe books over the years as an economical way to use up leftover or stale bread, nowadays it is served in many shapes and flavours. No longer is it just confined to simple layers of buttered bread and dried fruit, with beaten eggs and milk, but it now comes in various guises – with spices, orange or lemon flavourings, marmalade and even chocolate, all in an attempt to re-vitalise our taste for a timeless favourite. The dried fruit can be soaked in rum, brandy or sherry, and the pudding can be cooked in individual ramekins.

There are many local recipes for white-pot, such as those from the Fortescue family at Castle Hill, South Molton, Devon, and the Tremaynes at Heligan in South Cornwall.

Ingredients
3 oz (75 g) raisins and 1 oz (25 g) sultanas
2-3 tbsp rum
3 oz (75 g) sugar
1 tsp mixed spice, zest of 1 orange and few strands of saffron
6 slices thin white bread and butter
1 pint (575 ml) milk and 2 eggs
1 tbsp sugar and 1/2 tsp grated nutmeg

The night before, steep the saffron in a little hot water and soak the raisins and sultanas in the rum. The following day, cut the bread into triangles, and mix together the sugar and spices with the orange zest. Then in a large oval ovenproof dish (greased) layer the rum-soaked raisins and spiced sugar between the slices of white bread and butter, finishing with a layer of bread uppermost. Beat the eggs into the milk, add the soaked saffron and pour over the pudding, making sure that all the bread is covered by the liquid.

Sprinkle the surface with a little nutmeg and sugar, and leave to soak for at least 30 minutes before baking at 180°C/350°F/Gas

4 for 45 minutes or so, until well risen and golden brown. Serve straight from the oven whilst it is crisp and high, with cream or a thin pouring custard – or even with brandy butter (see page 29) as an indulgence.

Exeter pudding

Many different cakes and puddings are called after towns and cities: Helston pudding, Tiverton batter pudding, Clifton puffs and Bath buns spring to mind. Why Exeter pudding (which according to Mrs Beeton is 'very rich') is so named is a mystery.

Ingredients

1 oz (25 g) raisins, soaked overnight in rum

5 oz (150 g) breadcrumbs	3 oz (75 g) vegetable suet
3 oz (75 g) sugar	3 eggs
grated rind of 1 lemon	1/4 pint (150 ml) rum

4 oz (110 g) bramble jelly or similar

6 ratafia biscuits

For the sauce

2oz (50 g) bramble jelly warmed with 2 tbsp sherry

Soak the raisins overnight in the rum. The following day, beat the eggs and sugar together, then add the breadcrumbs, suet, lemon rind and rum, and mix well.

Grease a wide ovenproof dish and line the sides carefully with ratafia biscuits, pressing the raisins in between the biscuits. Spoon alternate layers of the creamed mixture with layers of bramble jelly, finishing with a layer of the egg mixture. Bake at 180°C/350°F/Gas 4 for 30-40 minutes, until the pudding is firm, well risen and golden in colour. Serve with a sauce made from bramble jelly, warmed in a little sherry.

Note The ratafia biscuits can be omitted, and the raisins scattered over the base of the dish, but the biscuits give the pudding a more decorative edge.

St Breock plum pudding

The British have always prided themselves on their dried fruit or suet puddings. In the eighteenth century it was quite common to indulge in three puddings, and by 1740 roast beef and plum pudding was regarded as the national dish.

The traditional plum or Christmas pudding began life as a plum pottage, a type of fruited porridge made with beef stock, which was then thickened with breadcrumbs and flavoured with spices and dried fruit. Sherry, port or orange juice were added just before serving. This plum pudding is based on an eighteenth-century recipe from St Breock, near Wadebridge in Cornwall.

Ingredients
12 oz (350 g) raisins
12 oz (350 g) currants
8 oz (225 g) sultanas
8 oz (225 g) mixed peel
12 oz (350 g) brown sugar
2 oz (50 g) chopped almonds
1 oz (25 g) ground almonds
12 oz (350 g) breadcrumbs
12 oz (350 g) suet
8 oz (225 g) flour, pinch of salt
2 tsp mixed spice
1/2 tsp cinnamon
1/4 tsp nutmeg
1/4 tsp cloves (ground)
3 eggs
2 tbsp treacle
3 tbsp brandy or rum
10 fl oz (275 ml) old ale, barley wine or home-made beer

Begin by soaking the dried fruit overnight in the ale and brandy. Early the next morning, mix all the dry ingredients together and then add the eggs and treacle with the fruit, brandy and ale. Place the mixture into about 5 well-greased pudding basins and boil, covered with well fitting lids or grease proof paper, for about 8 hours.

The pudding will keep until needed. Then boil it for a further 2 hours before serving with rum or brandy butter. (See below for rum and brandy butter recipes.)

Note Other ingredients can be added to the pudding, according to taste – a chopped apple or a small grated potato or carrot, for example. It is customary for all the family to take a turn at stirring the pudding to make sure the ingredients are well mixed and to have a wish at the same time.

Rum and brandy butter

A report on commercially made brandy butter, by *Good Housekeeping* in December 1996, said: 'Of the hundreds of different flavours and combinations that are available, we didn't find any that we were completely happy to recommend... We recommend that you make your own.'

On that note I suggest a Cornish recipe for brandy butter (given to me by Mrs Jackie Turnbull) to serve with the St Breock plum pudding. This is the recipe for the delicious brandy butter that accompanies the Christmas pudding served at the old persons' luncheon club Christmas Party in Mawnan Smith, Cornwall, each year – and the inspiration for this book!

Brandy butter ingredients
4 oz (110 g) butter   4 oz (110 g) sugar
1 tbsp sifted icing sugar   3-4 tbsp best brandy
2 tsp fresh orange juice

Make sure the butter and sugar are at room temperature. Beat well together until light and fluffy, then add 1 tbsp of sifted icing sugar. Measure out 3-4 tbsp of best brandy and just dribble into the mixture, beating well. Finally, add 2 tsp of fresh orange juice. Chill in the fridge before use.

Butter is said to symbolise the richness of life, sugar the sweetness, nutmeg the spice of life and, of course, rum the spirit. This next recipe for rum butter is said to have been concocted by some imaginative smugglers who were forced to hide from the Custom Men, in a cave off the coast. They managed to survive the enforced stay by mixing together their smuggled booty of rum, butter and sugar.

Rum butter ingredients

4 oz (110 g) unsalted butter	6 oz (175 g) caster sugar
1/2 grated nutmeg	1/4 tsp cinnamon
just under 2 fl oz (50 ml) rum	

Melt the butter gently over a low heat and then beat in the nutmeg, cinnamon and caster sugar until the crystals have been absorbed. Add the rum and beat well again. This quantity of nutmeg may appear to be excessive, but it is essential to the flavour. Grate from a whole nutmeg rather than using ready-grated nutmeg. Spoon into dainty glass dishes and, when cool, dredge with caster sugar. Cover and keep in the fridge until required.

Orange jelly

From the large number of cargoes of fruit washed up along the beaches after shipwrecks or captured by the Revenue officials in the course of their duties, it is obvious that exotic fruits had a place in seventeenth- and eighteenth-century cooking – there are many recipes in the local archives for orange and lemon jellies.

Also, the wealthier country estates had their own orangeries or glass houses where they could grow oranges, lemons and even pineapples for the table. The owners vied with one another as to who could produce the earliest fruit. The orangery at Saltram, for example, was built as early as 1771.

This practice of growing in heated conditions is being revived at The Lost Gardens of Heligan, near Mevagissey in South Cornwall, where melons and pineapples are now produced.

The Victorians were proud of their extensive range of decorated moulds and containers for jellies and creams, and they had cool dairies set apart from the busy, hot kitchens. Isinglas was the usual setting agent, but today we can use gelatine, or even commercial blocks of jelly, substituting part of the water with sherry or wine. Vegetarians can use agar flakes or gelozone.

Ingredients
4 tbsp or 1 oz (25 g) gelatine
1/2 pint (275 ml) water
1/2 pint (275 ml) sweet white wine
juice from three oranges and one lemon
1/4 pint (150 ml) whipped double cream
vanilla essence or 1 tsp rum

Warm the water just sufficiently to dissolve the gelatine and sugar and then add the wine, orange and lemon juice (one early nineteenth-century recipe from Devon suggests rubbing the sugar lumps over the oranges before dissolving the sugar in the jelly). Allow to set in a dampened fluted mould, overnight if possible. Turn out and serve with whipped cream, flavoured with a few drops of vanilla essence or 1 tsp rum.

Fruit salad

Gin, or 'geneva', was widely smuggled. Sloe gin is often made for drinking but gin in a fruit salad is more unusual, so your guests will be left guessing the source of the mystery taste.

Ingredients
Selection of fruits, exotic and home grown, such as: raspberries, strawberries, cubes of melon, halved black grapes (with the seeds removed) and a choice of Westcountry eating apples.

Cover with a sweet syrup made by boiling half a pint (275 ml) of water with 3 oz (75 g) sugar for a few minutes, and allow to cool. Spoon into individual dishes and pour 1 tbsp of Plymouth gin over each serving. Decorate with sprigs of mint.

1755: Churchwardens' accounts at Sithney in West Cornwall show that Margaret Foot, who was on Parish Relief, was allowed 1 1/2 gallons of brandy over twelve weeks. The cost at only 9 shillings a gallon suggests that it had been smuggled.

PASTRIES

A wide variety of puddings were made in pastry cases, and tarts (or tortes) were a useful base for many sweet and savoury dishes. Rum and brandy were added to all sorts of ingredients, such as potatoes, carrots, apples, apricots, lemons, oranges and mincemeat, as well as to egg custards. All in all, a riot of puddings, each enhanced with a splash of spirit.

Potato pudding

Established cookery writers gave recipes for Potato pudding, a type of curd tart (which is more interesting than its name suggests), thickened with potatoes and flavoured with lemon or nutmeg. It was served as a desert with wine sauce or as a side dish to accompany the meat.

Similar recipes appear in many Westcountry collections which use either wine or brandy. The following pudding is based on the ingredients in Mr William Blake's 1783 hand-written recipe book.

Ingredients

8 oz (225 g) short crust pastry
8 oz (225 g) cooked and mashed potatoes
4 oz (110 g) sugar
4 oz (110 g) butter
2 eggs
2 fl oz (50 ml) brandy
grated rind and juice from one lemon

First of all line a deep 8 inch (20 cm) pie plate with the pastry and put in a cool place whilst mixing the filling. Melt the butter over a gentle heat, then add the sugar and potatoes. Beat well and whisk in the eggs, lemon juice and brandy, making sure that all the ingredients are well mixed in. I find it's best to use a wire balloon whisk. After this, pour the filling into the pie dish and bake in a moderate oven at 180°C/350°F/Gas 4 for 45 minutes, until the pie is firm to touch.

Hot wine sauce

2 oz (50 g) butter   2 oz (50 g) sugar
8 fl oz (225 ml) sweet or dry white wine, according to taste
dash of lemon juice and 1 tbsp single cream to finish

Combine the ingredients and heat gently in a small pan.

Threshing Day tart

Traditionally, cloves, quinces and cinnamon are added to apple pies, but when the traveller and writer Celia Fiennes visited the Westcountry in 1698, she was intrigued by the Cornish method of baking an apple pie known as Threshing Day tart. The apples were placed in the dish, covered with pastry and baked in the usual manner and then, when cooked, the plate was inverted to reveal the steaming apples, sitting on the pastry. The complete pie was topped with clotted cream – perhaps spiced with rum.

In contrast, an eighteenth-century Devon recipe for an apple pudding, from the Guppy family of Sidbury, Budleigh Salterton, suggests cooking the apples, then adding eggs, flour, brandy, sugar, nutmeg and lemon peel before placing in a puff pastry case.

1698, Celia Fiennes wrote: 'my landlady brought me one of the West Country tarts, this was the first I met with, though I had asked for them in many places in Sommerset and Devonshire, its an apple pye with a custard all on the top... its a sort of clouted [clotted] cream as we call it, with a little sugar, and soe put on the top of the apple pye.'

Ingredients
8 oz (225 g) shortcrust pastry, flavoured with a little cinnamon
1½ lb (700 g) Westcountry cooking apples
4 oz (110 g) sugar, or to taste
6 cloves (optional)
8 oz (225 g) clotted cream flavoured with sugar and 2 tbsp rum

Prepare the fruit and place, with the sugar, in a circular pie dish. Cover with the pastry, rolling out a strip first of all to place around the rim - dampen it with cold water, then press the larger piece on to this. Decorate the edges with a fork.

Bake at 200°C/400°F/Gas 6 for 35-40 minutes. Remove from the oven, loosen the edges with a knife and leave to cool for 5 minutes, before turning upside down, with the apples on top.

Cover generously with clotted cream flavoured with rum.

Mincemeat pasty

No Westcountry recipe book would be complete without a pasty, but to be different here is a recipe for a sweet pasty, with mint and brandied mincemeat. Recipes for Christmas mincemeat date back to Elizabethan times, when a little chopped meat was usually added to the dried fruit. A typical recipe for mincemeat appears in the attractively written seventeenth-century recipe book from the Pendarves estate. It includes: beef suet, nutmeg, cinnamon, cloves, mace, salt, currants, raisins, pippins (apples), lemon – all mixed with 'a quarter of a pinte of brandy and halfe a pint of sack and halfe a pinte of white wine' and sugar. The following recipe is more modest.

Ingredients for each pasty
4 oz (110 g) shortcrust pastry
2 tbsp mincemeat
1 tsp chopped mint
1 tbsp brandy

Roll out the shortcrust pastry into four circles, with a plate as a guide, and fill each pasty with 2 tbsp of mincemeat, 1 tsp of chopped fresh mint and 1 tbsp of brandy. Dampen the edges, fold into the usual pasty shape, crimping the edges, and make 2 short slashes for the steam to escape. Glaze with beaten egg or milk and bake in a hot oven at 200°C/400°F/Gas 6 for about 15 minutes.

CAKES AND BISCUITS

Brandied gingerbread

Gingerbread is one of our oldest cakes and is said to have been baked by the Egyptians. Medieval gingerbread was made from honey-flavoured breadcrumbs that were then decorated with cloves and bay leaves, and often gilded – from which came the phrase 'the gilt on the gingerbread'. Gradually, as honey became more expensive, it was replaced by black treacle and, more recently, by golden syrup.

The coriander seeds originate from a Cornish source. The idea for putting brandy into gingerbread comes from the Guppy family recipe book, at Budleigh Salterton in Devon, and gives it a rich, full taste – try it for breakfast!

Ingredients

8 oz (225 g) flour	1/2 tsp salt
1/2 tsp bicarbonate of soda	1/2 tbsp ground ginger
1/2 tsp coriander seeds	4 oz (110 g) dark brown sugar
3 oz (75 g) cooking fat	3 oz (75 g) black treacle
3 oz (75 g) golden syrup	1 egg

just under 1/4 pint (150 ml) milk and made up to a total of
    1/4 pt (150 ml) with brandy

Mix the dry ingredients together in a bowl. Warm the fat, treacle and syrup until just melted, then stir in the sugar and add to the dry ingredients. Beat the egg into the milk and brandy, and add to the flour and treacle mixture. Pour into a lined 8 inch (20cm) x 12 inches (30cm) Swiss roll tin, and bake at 160°C/325°F/Gas 3 for 1/2 hour.

> 1739: In the early hours the *Lady Lucy* was wrecked at Gunwalloe, near Helston and by the time that the Custom Men appeared the cargo had disappeared – 68 tons of wine, 25 tons of coffee berries, 18 casks of indigo and 31 1/2 'pieces' of brandy. Some of the casks of wine were hidden away by the Vicar of Cury.

Cornish black cake or rich plum cake

Rich fruit cakes are even more delicious with any kind of spirit, be it brandy, whiskey or rum. The dried fruit becomes succulent and juicy, and the cake improves with keeping. In the past, fruit cakes were extremely large, with much dried fruit, and before the introduction of baking powder yeast was the usual raising agent.

There are many local recipes for fruit cakes, such as heavy cake, yeast or saffron cakes from Cornwall, and Blackmore Vale cake from Dorset – but probably the most typical is the Cornish black cake, which is dark and rich with fruit and resembles the Welsh bara brith or speckled bread.

Ingredients
8 oz (225 g) plain flour
pinch of salt
1 1/4 lb (600 g) mixed dried fruit (currants, raisins, sultanas)
1/4 tsp each ground nutmeg, cloves, ginger and cinnamon
4 oz (110 g) mixed peel
2 oz (50 g) chopped almonds
2 oz (50 g) chopped walnuts
6 oz (175 g) butter
6 oz (175 g) sugar
4 eggs
1 tsp bicarbonate of soda, dissolved in 1 tbsp warm milk
4 tbsp brandy

Line an 8 inch (20 cm) cake tin with greaseproof paper. Mix the dry ingredients together – flour, salt, fruit, nuts and spices.

Cream the butter in a large bowl and then add the sugar, beating until fluffy and light. Add the eggs, alternating with the dry ingredients, and finally add the bicarbonate of soda, milk and brandy. Spoon into the lined tin, smoothing the top and bake for 3-3$\frac{1}{2}$ hours – at 160°C/325°F/ Gas 3 for 1 hour and then at 140°C/275°F/Gas 1 for a further 2$\frac{1}{2}$ hours.

Note A bowl of water placed on the base of the oven helps the cake to retain moisture. To store, wrap it in greaseproof paper and soak with a glass of brandy from time to time.

Spiced saffron tea bread

The taxation of tea has always been an emotive issue: the Boston Tea Party of 1773 and the break up of the American Colonies revolved around this everyday drink.

In the grand houses, the lady of the house or housekeeper would keep the tea under lock and key, while in ordinary households tea (unless smuggled) was even scarcer.

According to one Westcountry account, it was a special treat to be given 'a drink of tea right out of the tea-pot'. Coffee and chocolate were also subject to tax and were sold on the black market, but for drinking rather than for cooking.

Reminders of smuggling days are still to be seen along the Westcountry coastline, with the Tea Caverns at Newquay and Brandy Cove near Torbay.

---

22 July 1816, *Sherborne Mercury*: wreck of the *Jonge Anthony*, Porthleven [14 July], with a cargo of tea, salt and cocoa – 'Of the 1300 chests of tea which were on board, about 500 have been secured... it is supposed that more than that number have been secreted by the people near the coast, as of the 500 saved, nearly 200 were discovered in a barn... placed by the plunderers who swarmed about the vessel.'

The loaf in this recipe is fatless, but the rum gives good keeping quality.

Ingredients
1/2 sachet of powdered saffron or 30 saffron filaments
4 tbsp rum
1/4 pint (150 ml) cold tea
4 oz (110 g) sugar
8 oz (225 g) mixed dried fruit
1 egg
8 oz (225 g) self-raising flour
1/2 tsp ground ginger
1/4 grated nutmeg

Leave the sugar and fruit, saffron and 2 tbsp of rum to soak overnight in the tea. The next day, stir well and add the beaten egg, spices and the flour, mixing all the ingredients well together. Put into a lined loaf tin (1 1/2 lb/700 g) and bake at 160°C/325°F/ Gas 3 for 70 minutes. Turn out on to a wire rack to cool, but whilst still warm spike the base of the cake in a few places with a sharp fork and pour over the remaining 2 tbsp of rum to plump up the fruit.

Lemon whiskey cake

Every cake is a celebration, especially when it is made with smuggled Irish whiskey. Such a recipe appears in Catherine Rothwell's book *Old Cornish Recipes*, on which this lemon whiskey cake is

During the 1760s and 1770s William Rawlings, a wine merchant from St Columb in North Cornwall, wrote repeatedly to the President of the Board of Trade, pointing out how honest business men could not compete against smugglers. West Indian rum, he said, was available all over Cornwall at 5 shillings a gallon, whereas he had to sell it at 8 shillings and 6 pence.

based. It has a rich, crumbly finish but the whiskey-flavoured butter cream holds it all together.

Ingredients
8 oz (225 g) raisins
5 fl oz (150 ml) water
4 oz (110 g) butter
5 oz (150 g) sugar
6 oz (175 g) flour
1 egg
1/2 tsp ground nutmeg
1 tsp of bicarbonate of soda
3 oz (75 g) chopped walnuts
grated rind and juice from half a lemon
3 tbsp whiskey

Grease and line the base of two 8 inch (20 cm) sandwich tins. Put the raisins into a pan with the water and simmer gently for 15 minutes.

Meanwhile, cream the butter and sugar well together and beat in the egg.

Sieve the flour and nutmeg, and add to the creamed mixture with the raisins, walnuts and water.

Finally add the grated lemon rind, juice, bicarbonate and the whiskey. Pour into the tins and bake in a moderate oven at 180°C/350°F/Gas 4 for 40-45 minutes. Ice and fill with butter cream.

Butter cream ingredients
3 oz (75 g) butter
8 oz (225 g) icing sugar
3 tbsp of whiskey

Cream the butter and sugar together and then mix in the whiskey, beating well until smooth. Fill the centre of the cake with a little apricot jam and butter cream, swirling the remaining cream over the top.

In his autobiography, the travel writer John Silk Buckingham (1786-1855) described a smuggler's funeral at Breage, near Helston, in 1793. The guests were treated to a glass of brandy on arrival as well as between courses and the meal finished with plentiful supplies of tobacco, brandy, rum and gin.

Tipsy cake

A tipsy cake was a favourite at large social gatherings or balls, when a plain sponge cake would be soaked with sherry, Madeira or Marsala, then covered with whipped cream and spiked with split almonds. Perhaps it is the fore-runner of our present day trifle; Eliza Acton writes in her cookery book, in 1845, that rich, cold custard can be poured around the tipsy cake. The Victorians added butter to the sponge, which gave us our present-day Victoria sandwich cake.

There are many old local recipes for such cakes but it is difficult to link the cake recipes of smuggling times to modern needs. The quantities are huge and the instructions impractical. Writing in the eighteenth century, Mrs Carew from Antony House, for example, uses 'the yolks of 12 eggs and the whites of 8'. Then we are told to 'stir it well with a wooden spoon for an hour and a half, observing to stir it one way... then put it into a stew pan or any other convenient thing.' A modern version is given instead!

Ingredients for sponge cake
3 oz (75 g) self-raising flour   pinch of salt
2 eggs   3 oz (75 g) sugar

To finish
5 fl oz (150 ml) sherry or Madeira
10 fl oz (275 ml) double cream
2 oz (50 g) flaked almonds
4 oz (110 g) apricot jam

Grease and base line two 8 inch (20 cm) sandwich tins with

greaseproof paper (or you can just sprinkle the greased base with 1 dsp of sifted flour and sugar).

Place a mixing bowl over a pan of boiling water and break the eggs into the bowl. Add the sugar and whisk together until the mixture thickens. Remove from the heat and continue whisking until the whisk leaves a trail in the egg and sugar mixture. Carefully fold in the sieved flour and salt with a metal spoon and pour the mixture into the prepared tins. Bake at just a little above 180°C/350°F/Gas 4 for 20 minutes or so, until firmly risen. Turn the sponge cakes on to a wire rack to cool.

Fill the cooled cake with apricot jam, then cut out a circle from the top of the cake and fill with 1/4 pint (150 ml) of sweet sherry Leave the sherry to soak in overnight, spooning the liquid over the cake as necessary.

Before serving, replace the cut out piece of sponge, cover the cake with whipped cream and decorate with flaked almonds.

Easter biscuits

Easter biscuits were traditionally served to the children on Easter Sunday, to entice them into church. They can be made with currants or other dried fruit, with different spices, and sometimes they are iced and sandwiched together. Unlike modern biscuits, they are thick and chewy and a real favourite with children.

Easter biscuits are said to come from Devon, but this particular recipe is from Sedgemoor in Somerset.

Ingredients

8 oz (225 g) plain flour	pinch of salt
4 oz (110 g) butter	4 oz (110 g) sugar
1/2 tsp cinnamon	1/4 tsp ginger
1/4 tsp nutmeg	3 oz (75 g) currants
1 egg	2 tbsp brandy

Sieve the flour and salt together and rub in the fat until the mixture resembles fine breadcrumbs. Stir in the sugar, currants and spices. Beat the egg with the brandy and stir into the dry ingredients, kneading into a soft dough. Roll out on a well floured board, cutting into biscuit rounds about half an inch (1¹/4 cm) thick, using a 2¹/2 inch (6.5 cm) cutter.

Put the biscuits on to a greased baking sheet and bake in a medium oven at 180°C/350°F/Gas 4 for 15-20 minutes or until golden brown.

CHEESE

There are many excellent Westcountry cheeses available today, but most are of recent origin.

Cheese making on a large commercial scale only started towards the end of the nineteenth century. So it came as a surprise to me to find that there is a recipe for slipcoat cheese, a curd cheese wrapped in nettles, in one of the Antony House (at Torpoint) eighteenth-century recipe books – perhaps the forerunner of Yarg? (Cornish Yarg has only been produced since 1983 and Devon Tala cheese dates from 1987, although Cheddar and Dorset Blue Vinney have longer pedigrees.)

Until relatively recently, cheese, especially curd cheese, was made in the farmhouse kitchen and most of the grand houses had their own cool, tiled dairy. Thomas Hardy is said to have described Blackmore Vale in Dorset as 'the Vale of little dairies'.

Potted cheese

Different cheeses and leftovers can be used and the alcohol ensures keeping quality in this traditional Westcountry recipe.

In 1860 Mrs Beeton wrote:
'Cheese, in its commonest shape, is only fit for sedentary people, as an after-dinner stimulant; and in very small quantity. Bread and cheese, as a meal, is only fit for soldiers on the march or labourers in the open air.'

Ingredients
8 oz (225 g) grated Cheddar or similar cheese
2 oz (50 g) unsalted butter
1/2 tsp each of dry mustard powder and ground nutmeg
1/4 tsp cayenne pepper
2 tbsp brandy
2 tbsp melted butter
few walnut halves for decoration

Cream and pound the butter and cheese together with the dry ingredients, then gradually work in the brandy. Spoon carefully into small pots and cover with melted butter.

When cold, decorate with walnut halves. Serve on toast or as a sandwich filling.

Curd cheese cakes

Curd cheese cakes made with dried fruit, sugar and spices, and then baked in a pastry case, were a common sweet course dish during the eighteenth century.

There are many Westcountry recipes for curd cheese cakes, either with or without the pastry, and the following is based on a seventeenth-century recipe. It has a real old-fashioned taste about it, spicy and not over-sweet.

The curd cheese was usually made overnight, with rennet, or as the recipe book from the Tremayne (Heligan) family suggests 'Made in the morning, ready for dinner'. Sieved cottage cheese or soft cream cheese can be substituted.

Ingredients for curd cheese
1 pint (575 ml) milk
3 tbsp rennet (vegetarian rennet is available if preferred)

To make curd cheese, warm one pint of milk to blood temperature (37^0 C or 98.4^0F), adding the rennet to ensure a good set. Then allow the set curd to drain through a clean tea towel or muslin for several hours or overnight to remove the whey.

Ingredients for curd cheese cakes
2 oz (50 g) fresh white breadcrumbs
5 fl oz (150 ml) full cream milk
12 oz (350 g) curd cheese, cream cheese or
    sieved cottage cheese
2 oz (50 g) sugar
3 eggs
2 tbsp double cream
2 tbsp brandy – although rum or whiskey are equally suitable
3 oz (75 g) currants
2 tsp cinnamon
1 tsp ground nutmeg
12 oz (325 g) shortcrust pastry

Put the breadcrumbs and milk in a small saucepan and bring to the boil. Cook for a few minutes, until thick. Allow to cool, but not to go completely cold. Meanwhile, mix together the curd or cream cheese, sugar, brandy, eggs, cream, currants and spices, and add to the cooled breadcrumbs. With the prepared pastry, line about 20 deep patty tins (the number will depend on the size of the tins) and fill with the mixture. If you have too much mixture for your pastry cases, the curd cheese can be baked in small ramekins, like mini Yorkshire puddings. Bake at 180°C/350°F/Gas 4 for about 1/2 hour. The heat should be reduced if the curd cheese browns too quickly and the timing depends on the depth of the mixture. Serve with any Westcountry clotted cream.

30 September 1837: *Le Landais* was grounded off a small cove near Cape Cornwall. It was reported that cases of wines and cordials lay scattered along the sands and the leaking casks filled the rock pools and crevices with best brandy. Tinners, fishermen and labourers, together with their wives and families, descended on the wreck and, after two days, the Preventive Men had to retreat. Years later, bottles from *Le Landais* were still stacked away in cottages around St Just.

PRESERVES

Apple, pear and plum trees have a long history in the Westcountry: the soil and climate suit them well. There is even a rare Plymouth pear which is now an endangered species, because it is not self-pollinating. Commercial cider making is usually associated with Somerset and Devon, but at one time there were apple orchards in most villages in the South West. Many different local varieties were grown by the gentry, with such strange names as 'Pig's Nose' or 'Snell's Glass Apple' – in 1840, for example, the Fox family at Glendurgan, beside the sheltered Helford River, were growing some 78 varieties of apple. To remedy the decline of the local apples, the recently formed 'Orchard Project' in Cornwall has been encouraging the re-planting of the former apple orchards along the Tamar and other sheltered river valleys and to date some 56 old varieties have been re-established.

Apple jelly

A recipe for using up the surfeit of windfall apples, with the brandy giving keeping quality – and it also helps it to set. There is a clearly written out 'receipt' for Devon apple jelly in a book dated 1829-30. The suggested flavourings are cloves, cochineal and saffron, although I find that a handful of blackberries does just as well and gives the jelly a rich, warm red colour.

Ingredients
4 lb (1.8 kg) windfall apples, cookers or eaters
handful of blackberries, to give colour
3 pints (1.75 litres) water
1 lb (450 g) sugar for each pint (575 ml) of juice
1/2 oz (15 g) butter
1 tbsp lemon juice
1 tbsp brandy for each jar

Wash and clean the fruit, removing any bruised or damaged

flesh. If large, chop the apples into quarters, but there is no need to peel the fruit. Place in a large preserving pan with the blackberries and water, and stew gently until soft and pulpy. This will take about 2 hours or even longer. Strain the fruit through a large jelly bag, piece of muslin or old tea towel, and leave to drip overnight. It is important not to force the apples through the muslin, otherwise the finished jelly will be cloudy.

The next morning measure out the ruby red juice and allow 1 lb (450 g) of sugar for every pint (575 ml) of juice. Add the lemon juice at this stage: as we are told in the Devon recipe book, 'the more lemon juice the better it will jelly'.

Stir until the sugar dissolves and then boil rapidly for about 20 minutes, until you get a good set. You can test the setting point by dropping some of the liquid on to a cold saucer. If you can push the jelly into ridges when cool, it is ready for bottling. Longer boiling at this stage does not produce better jelly; overboiling gives a thick, treacly substance.

Remove the scum with a metal spoon or float a knob of butter in the hot jelly which will dispel most of it. Bottle whilst hot, adding a tablespoon of best brandy to each jar.

Pears in red wine

The Cornwall Record Office have an interesting collection of recipes dated 1860, written out by Mary Dingle, wife of the mathematician William Grylls Adams.

It includes a recipe for preserved pears with wine, on which the following is based.

Ingredients

8 small Conference pears	1 lemon
4oz (110g) sugar	1/2 tsp ginger
3 cloves	1/2 tsp cinnamon
few drops of cochineal	1/4 pt (150ml) red wine
1/4 pt (150ml) water	

Peel and core the pears 'with a silver knife' and cut the lemon into thin slices. Add the spices and lemon to the wine and water, mix in the cochineal and sugar, and boil over a gentle heat until the sugar has dissolved.

Add the pears and poach until tender. Conference pears will need to be cooked for about 20 minutes, although other varieties need less time.

Take out the pears and place in suitable containers.

Increase the heat and boil the liquid in the pan until it thickens. Remove the lemon slices and pour the syrup over the pears.

Brandied peaches

Peaches are regularly grown both indoors and outdoors in the favourable climate of the Westcountry. As indicated in a seventeenth-century recipe book, they can be preserved well in brandy.

Ingredients
6 peaches
4 oz (110 g) sugar
sufficient brandy to cover peaches

Plunge the peaches into boiling water for a few seconds, without letting them boil.

Remove and refresh them in cold water, then drain. Carefully peel the peaches and place in 'wide mouthed bottles'.

Sprinkle with 4 oz (110 g) sugar and fill up the bottles with brandy. Shake gently until the sugar has dissolved and keep for at least a month before using.

INDEX OF RECIPES